WORSHIP KIDS COLLECTION

Presents

Whom Shall I Fear

(God of Angel Armies)

12 Modern Worship Songs for Kids Choir!

Produced by
Jeff Sandstrom

Available Products:
Choral Book.. 45757-2411-7
CD Preview Pak 45757-2411-1
Listening CD 45757-2411-2
Split-Track Accompaniment CD 45757-2411-3
Split-Track Accompaniment DVD (2 Disc Set) 45757-2411-6
(Disc #1 - Standard Split-Track DVD, Disc #2 - DVD Rom with .MOV Files)

www.brentwoodbenson.com | www.worshiptogether.com

 a division of BRENTWOOD·BENSON music publications in association with WORSHIP TOGETHER

© MMXIV Brentwood-Benson Music Publications, 101 Winners Circle, Brentwood, TN 37027. All Rights Reserved. Unauthorized Duplication Prohibited.

CONTENTS

God Who Saves 3

Always Will 14

Whom Shall I Fear (God of Angel Armies) 26

10,000 Reasons (Bless the Lord) 36

White Flag 46

Awake My Soul 57

God's Great Dance Floor 67

In Jesus' Name 76

One Thing Remains (Your Love Never Fails) 86

Victor's Crown 94

Sing and Shout 104

This Beating Heart 115

God Who Saves

Words and Music by
SAM KNOCK
Arranged by Jeff Sandstrom

Whom Shall I Fear
(God of Angel Armies)

Words and Music by
CHRIS TOMLIN, ED CASH
and SCOTT CASH
Arranged by Jeff Sandstrom

Awake My Soul

57

Words and Music by
CHRIS TOMLIN, DANIEL CARSON,
JASON INGRAM and JESSE REEVES
Arranged by Jeff Sandstrom

© Copyright 2012 (Arr. © Copyright 2013) worshiptogether.com Songs / sixsteps Music (ASCAP) / Worship Together Music / Sixsteps Songs /
A Thousand Generations Publishing (BMI) (Administered at CapitolCMGPublishing.com) / Sony/ATV Music Publishing LLC /
Open Hands Music (SESAC). Sony/ATV Music Publishing LLC / Open Hands Music administered by Sony/ATV Music Publishing LLC
(8 Music Square West, Nashville, TN 37203). All rights reserved. Used by permission. *Reprinted by permission of Hal Leonard Corporation.*
PLEASE NOTE: Copying of this music is NOT covered by the CCLI license. For CCLI information call 1-800-234-2446.

SCRIPTURE READING:

⁴ Then he said to me, "Prophesy to these bones and say to them, 'Dry bones, hear the word of the LORD! ⁵ This is what the Sovereign LORD says to these bones: I will make breath enter you, and you will come to life.'"

⁷ So I prophesied as I was commanded. And as I was prophesying, there was a noise, a rattling sound, and the bones came together, bone to bone. ⁸ I looked, and tendons and flesh appeared on them and skin covered them, but there was no breath in them.

⁹ Then he said to me, "Prophesy to the breath; prophesy, son of man, and say to it, … 'Come from the four winds, O breath, and breathe …'" *(Ezekiel 37:4,5,7-9a NIV)*

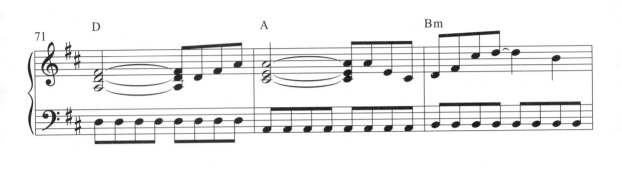

RAP:
I'm not alone, I realize. I breathe out. I come alive.
Your Word gives life to my dry bones.
Your breath tells death it can ride on.
Awake me, make me a living stone, a testament to Your throne, I…
I'm nothing without You – I'm on my own –
The only One who satisfies my soul.

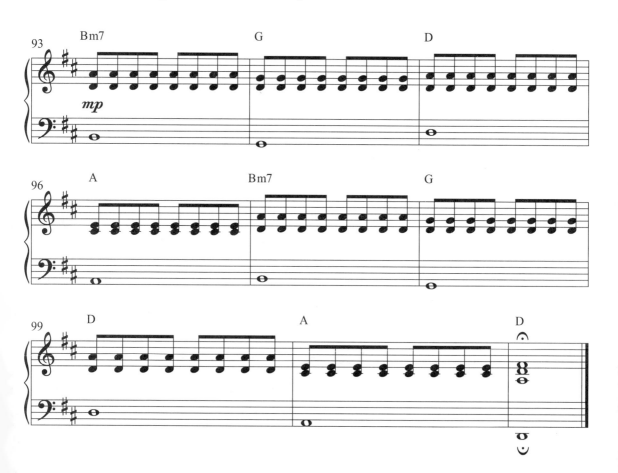

In Jesus' Name

Words and Music by
DARLENE ZSCHECH
and ISRAEL HOUGHTON
Arranged by Jeff Sandstrom

© Copyright 2013 Integrity Worship Music / Darlene Zschech Co-Pub (ASCAP) / Integrity's Praise! Music / Sound of the New Breed (BMI)
(Administered at CapitolCMGPublishing.com). All rights reserved. Used by permission.
PLEASE NOTE: Copying of this music is NOT covered by the CCLI license. For CCLI information call 1-800-234-2446.

This Beating Heart

Words and Music by
JONAS MYRIN and MATT REDMAN
Arranged by Jeff Sandstrom

© Copyright 2013 Thankyou Music (PRS) (Administered worldwide at CapitolCMGPublishing.com excluding Europe which is administered at weareworship.com) / Shout! Music Publishing (APRA) (Administered in the US and Canada at CapitolCMGPublishing.com) / worshiptogether.com Songs / Sixsteps Music / Said and Done Music (ASCAP) (Administered at CapitolCMGPublishing.com). All rights reserved. Used by permission.

PLEASE NOTE: Copying of this music is NOT covered by the CCLI license. For CCLI information call 1-800-234-2446.

JOIN
THE BRENTWOOD KIDS MUSIC CLUB

AND RECEIVE OUR NEW MUSIC RELEASES FOR AN ENTIRE YEAR FROM TOP ARRANGERS: DENNIS & NAN ALLEN, JEFF SANDSTROM, RHONDA FRAZIER, ED KEE, ANNETTE ODEN, JOHNATHAN CRUMPTON, LUKE GAMBILL, PAM ANDREWS AND MANY MORE!

As an exclusive member of this amazing Kids Music Resource, you will receive:

- A wide variety of new, energetic and exciting Kids music delivered straight to your door 4-5 times each year. This includes seasonal and non-seasonal musicals, collections and great DVD resources for Kids Choir, VBS, Summer Camp or Sunday School. **(That's over $150.00 in music!)**
- Complete songbooks, audio recordings and DVD samplers – no excerpts!
- 15% discount on all choral books, listening CD's and CD/DVD accompaniment tracks.
- Share the Music magazine containing new release information, informative articles, activities and games for your kids, teaching tips and special offers for Brentwood Kids Music Club members only!
- Choral Music Specialists available to assist you with product information.
- 24 hour on-line ordering with special offers exclusively for club members.
- A FREE music voucher for purchase of music product!

CALL 1-800-846-7664 TODAY
AND LET US DO ALL THE WORK FOR YOU.
WE WILL ONLY SEND YOU OUR VERY BEST!

BOBKCCTEN

Check Out These Amazing DVD Resources For Kids!

Perfect For Kids Choir, Children's Church, Sunday School, VBS, Summer Camp or for Any Time Of The Year.

NOW ONLY $19.99 EA.

Kids Resource DVDs
DVDs contain individual videos or fun background images with lyrics so that your kids can sing along or enter into worship! (*motions included on Crazy Praize titles*)

Kids Demonstration DVDs
DVDs show complete full-scale productions of these musicals or collections!

Call **1-800-846-7664** or order online @ **www.brentwoodbenson.com** or call your local Christian Bookstore today!

essential KIDZ Resource DVD

A FUN Resource to enhance your kids' worship serivce!

CALL TODAY FOR A FREE DVD SAMPLER!

This DVD resource includes:
- Praise & Worship - 8 great songs with exciting visuals and onscreen lyrics. Songs include: *Big House, King of the Jungle, His Cheeseburger, Every Move I Make* and more!
- Count Downs - 2 visual count downs to let your kids know when service begins.
- Birthday Songs – 2 new fun birthday songs with full-mix and split trax options.
- Segment Title Screens - Includes: Praise & Worship, Game Time, Tithes & Offerings, Memory Verse, Prayer Time, Quiet Time, and Story Time.

Call **Brentwood-Benson** today at **1-800-846-7664**
or visit us on line at
www.BrentwoodBenson.com

DISCOVER MORE GREAT KIDS MUSICALS
FROM THE BRENTWOOD KIDS MUSIC CLUB!

Down by the Creek Bank

Can you believe it? Down By the Creek Bank is 25 years old this year! It's a timeless Classic for kids of all ages! Introduce a new generation to Down By the Creek Bank and watch your kids have even more fun than you did 25 years ago! So, grab a fishin' pole and a friend and join us for the most fun 35 minutes anyone can have "by the old, holler log!"

The Tale of Three Trees

The Tale of Three Trees brings to life this children's Classic - a story of some trees with a dream, and a God with a plan. Through the hopes and dreams of three trees, we are reminded that even when we can't see the forest for the trees, there is no prayer too big or too small for God!

We Are United

Unify your children's choir as they "survive" the challenges of Henotes Island in We Are United, a musical island adventure featuring fun original songs your kids will love performing. Based on the 1 Corinthians 12:12-27 theme "one body, many parts," six castaways compete on the island to win the "grand prize," only to discover that the real way to win is to work together as one in Christ.

Call 1-800-846-7664, visit www.brentwoodbenson.com or order from your local Christian retailer today!

My First PIANO BOOK
worship songs & Hymns

Only $14.99 each

Beginner Piano Arrangements by David Thibodeaux

* Volume 1 - Worship Songs
* Volume 2 - Worship Songs
* Volume 3 - Worship Songs
* Volume 1 - Hymns
* Volume 2 - Hymns

Plus 17 Christmas Favorites!
by David Thibodeaux

* **My First Piano Book Christmas Songs**
  Songs include: O Little Town of Bethlehem
  * Away in the Manger * Carol of the Bells
  * Deck the Halls * Mary, Did You Know?
  * Go, Tell It On the Mountain * Isn't He? * Jingle Bells
  * Joy to the World * Angels We Have Heard on High
  * O Come, All Ye Faithful * Silent Night, Holy Night
  * The Twelve Days of Christmas * Up on the Housetop
  * We Wish You A Merry Christmas * What Child is This?
  * Rudolph, the Red-Nosed Reindeer

BRENTWOOD-BENSON music publishing

Call **1-800-846-7664**, www.brentwoodbenson.com
or visit **your local Christian Retailer** and purchase your books today**!**